Date: 12/14/15

J BIO CURRY
Fishman, Jon M.
Stephen Curry /

Stephen Curry

By Jon M. Fishman

AMAZING ATHLETES

Lerner Publications ◆ Minneapolis

Lerner Publications Company
A division of Lerner Publishing Group, Inc.
241 First Avenue North
Minneapolis, MN 55401 USA

For reading levels and more information, look up this title at www.lernerbooks.com.

Library of Congress Cataloging-in-Publication Data

Fishman, Jon M.
    Stephen Curry / by Jon M. Fishman.
        pages cm
    Includes bibliographical references and index.
    ISBN 978-1-4677-7921-0 (lb : alk. paper) — ISBN 978-1-4677-8112-1 (pb : alk. paper) —
ISBN 978-1-4677-8545-7 (eb pdf)
    1. Curry, Stephen, 1988—Juvenile literature. 2. Basketball players—United States—
Biography—Juvenile literature. I. Title.
    GV884.C88F57 2016
    796.323092—dc23   2015013547

Manufactured in the United States of America
1 – BP – 7/15/15

TABLE OF CONTENTS

Stephen Curry dribbles past Devin Harris of the Dallas Mavericks.

SUPERMAN

Stephen Curry and the Golden State Warriors were losing to the Dallas Mavericks on February 4, 2015. Dallas had been hot since the opening **tip-off**. Golden State looked slow on their feet. Early in the first quarter, the

Mavericks had a huge lead, 24–4.

Golden State coach Steve Kerr didn't panic. He knew that with Stephen on the team, the Warriors would never be too far behind to catch up. "Sometimes Steph plays his best when we're down big, and he just senses that he has to put the Superman cape on," Kerr said.

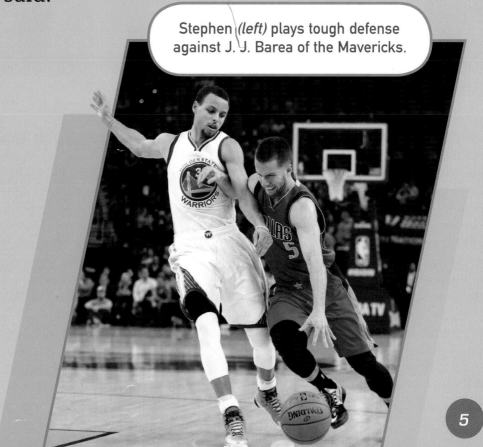

Stephen *(left)* plays tough defense against J. J. Barea of the Mavericks.

Golden State Warriors
coach Steve Kerr *(right)*

In the second quarter, the Warriors slowly chipped away at Dallas's lead. By halftime, Golden State was down by only 4 points, 62–58.

In the third quarter, Stephen and his teammates didn't look so slow on their feet. They flew around the court. The Warriors began running a play called the **pick-and-roll**.

A teammate would pass the ball to Stephen and then stand in one place to create a pick. Stephen would run, or roll, close to the teammate. Stephen's **defender** would then have to follow Stephen around the player creating the pick, giving Stephen space to take an open shot. "It's my favorite [kind of play]," Stephen said.

The pick-and-roll often created a bit of open space for Stephen to shoot. And he didn't need much room to take a good shot. In the second half of the game, Stephen nailed basket after basket. In the third quarter alone, he made six **three-point field goals** and scored 26 total points.

Stephen won the three-point field goal contest at the 2015 NBA All-Star Game. In the final round, he made 13 three-pointers in a row.

Stephen *(right)* looks for a shot past the Mavericks' Al-Farouq Aminu.

Golden State beat Dallas, 128–114. Stephen had scored 51 points in the game. No one else on his team scored more than 18 points. "He had one of those extra-special nights," Dallas coach Rick Carlisle said. "I've never seen anybody in this league hit shots like that."

Stephen *(right)* with his family

NBA FAMILY

On March 14, 1988, Wardell Stephen Curry II was born in Akron, Ohio. His friends and family called him Steph from the time he was small. He grew up with his younger brother, Seth, and younger sister, Sydel. The Currys lived in Ohio when Steph was born because his father, Dell,

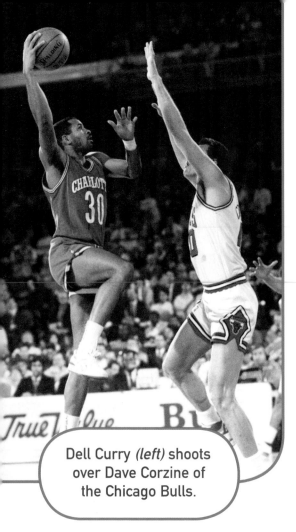

Dell Curry *(left)* shoots over Dave Corzine of the Chicago Bulls.

played for the NBA's Cleveland Cavaliers. After the 1987–1988 season, Dell switched teams. The family moved to Charlotte, North Carolina, where Dell played for the Charlotte Hornets.

Steph's mother, Sonya, had played three sports in high school. As a college student at Virginia Tech University, she played on the women's volleyball team. With two athletic parents, it was natural that Steph loved sports. But Dell and Sonya made sure their kids focused on being kids rather than NBA stars. "During the week I tried to keep [the kids] home when Dell had games because their job was school," Sonya said. "Then on the weekends, they got to go to games."

Dell spent a lot of time traveling to other cities for games while the rest of the family stayed in Charlotte. Sonya often had to care for the three children by herself.

Dell holds many Charlotte Hornets all-time records, including the most points scored in a career.

Steph was named after his dad, whose full name is Wardell Stephen Curry I.

Steph's sister says he was a "goofball" as a child and loved to joke around.

"With my dad being on the road a lot, she did a great job with me and my [brother and sister]," Steph said. "She deserves a lot of credit for how we turned out."

Like his father, Steph was a skilled basketball player. He could **dribble** and shoot like a much older boy. But he also enjoyed football and baseball. In seventh grade, Steph thought about quitting basketball to focus on baseball. "It wasn't like I always wanted to be a pro basketball player," he said. He later decided not to give up the sport.

After the 1997–1998 NBA season, Dell moved to a new team again. This time, he went to Milwaukee, Wisconsin, to play for the Bucks. He played one season for the Bucks before agreeing to join the Toronto Raptors beginning in 1999. The Currys moved to Toronto, Canada.

Dell *(left)* makes his way around Antoine Walker of the Boston Celtics.

Toronto is the capital of Ontario, Canada.

LEARNING TO SHOOT AGAIN

In 2001, Steph began attending a middle school called Queensway Christian College in Toronto. The eighth grader was quiet and slim and barely stood over 5 feet tall. He didn't look like the son of an NBA player to Queensway basketball coach James Lackey. But Steph quickly proved that he didn't need to be big to be a good player. "He was this tiny little guy, but when we put him on the court he was just unbelievable," Lackey said. Steph's team didn't lose a game all season.

Steph was the best shooter on his team. But his father didn't like the way his son shot the ball. Dell thought Steph held the ball too low before letting it go. Steph's shooting style worked well against other eighth graders.

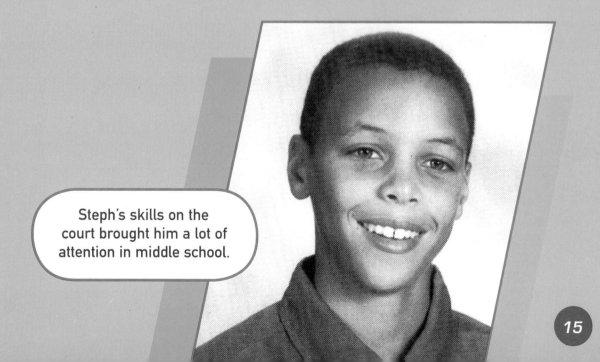

Steph's skills on the court brought him a lot of attention in middle school.

Steph poses with a friend in this photo from his high school days.

But as he grew older, players on other teams would learn to block those shots.

Dell helped change the way Steph shot a basketball. Instead of holding it near his hip before shooting, Steph worked on holding the ball over his head. That would make it harder for other players to reach to block his shots. But changing his shot wasn't easy. Steph practiced for weeks before he felt comfortable with the new style.

After the 2001–2002 season, Dell retired

from the NBA. The family moved back to Charlotte. In 2002, Steph started at Charlotte Christian School as a high school

freshman. He was still small for his age, but his basketball skills were sharper than ever.

By his junior year in 2004–2005, Steph was the star of the **varsity** team. That season, Charlotte Christian played a tough game against West Charlotte High School.

Dell watches his son Steph play basketball.

West Charlotte played with a style called a **full-court press**. The style can make it hard for the other team to move the ball down the court. But Steph wasn't bothered by the press. "I just remember . . . Steph being completely able to handle it," said teammate Ben Walton.

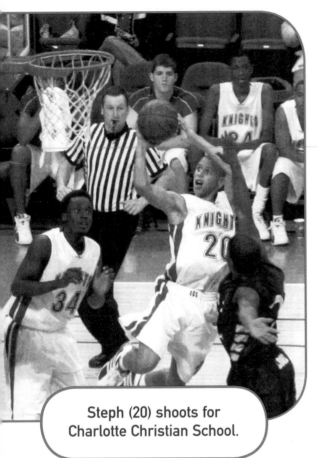

Steph (20) shoots for Charlotte Christian School.

Steph *(second from right)* smiles alongside his family on Senior Signing Day, when high school athletes sign with college teams.

BIG ENOUGH

Steph's basketball talents impressed his coaches and teammates. He used his fast feet and smooth dribbling skills to break full-court presses. He gave all his effort on defense. And he sank deep baskets using the style his father had taught him.

Steph dressed his best for this photo from his high school yearbook.

It was time for Steph to think about going to college. But some college **scouts** thought Steph shot the ball too often instead of passing to teammates. Other scouts didn't think Steph was tall enough or strong enough to play college basketball. In 2005, he stood about 5 feet 11. "He was such a late bloomer," Sonya said. "He didn't look the part [of a college basketball player]. We heard the negative comments: 'He's not big enough.'"

Steph had hoped that his basketball abilities would help him earn a **scholarship**. But the schools with the best basketball teams weren't especially interested in him. Virginia Tech, where Dell and Sonya had gone to college, offered to let Steph join their team as a **walk-on**. Walk-on players must pay for school themselves and may be cut from the team before the season starts. Steph turned down the offer.

Davidson College is about 20 miles north of Charlotte, North Carolina. The college is small and doesn't usually play against bigger

Steph attended Davidson College in Davidson, North Carolina.

schools such as Virginia Tech. Davidson Wildcats basketball coaches Bob McKillop and Matt Matheny had been trying to convince Steph to join their team for more than a year. In September 2005, the coaches drove to Steph's house and offered him a scholarship. He accepted, and McKillop and Matheny were thrilled. "Coach and I were dancing in the living room," Matheny said.

Steph proved right away that his coaches

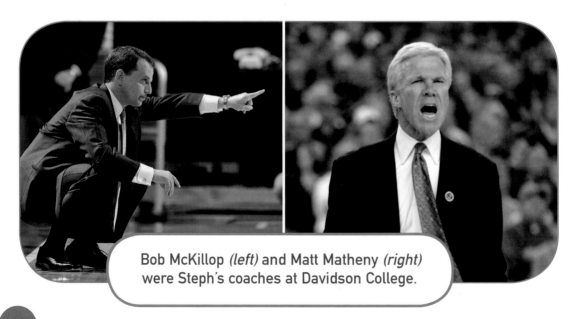

Bob McKillop (left) and Matt Matheny (right) were Steph's coaches at Davidson College.

had good reason to dance. In 2006–2007, Steph scored 730 points, an incredible total for a freshman. It was more points than any other player in the **conference** that season! The Wildcats were invited to play in the **National Collegiate Athletic Association (NCAA)** basketball **tournament**. But Steph and his teammates couldn't keep up with the University of Maryland in the first round. Davidson lost the game, 82–70.

Davidson is one of the oldest colleges in North Carolina. It has been a school since 1837.

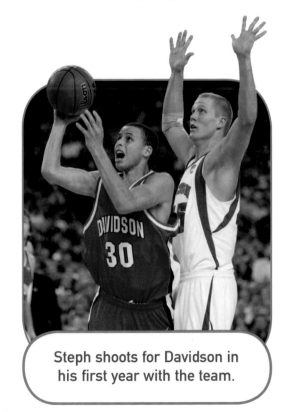

Steph shoots for Davidson in his first year with the team.

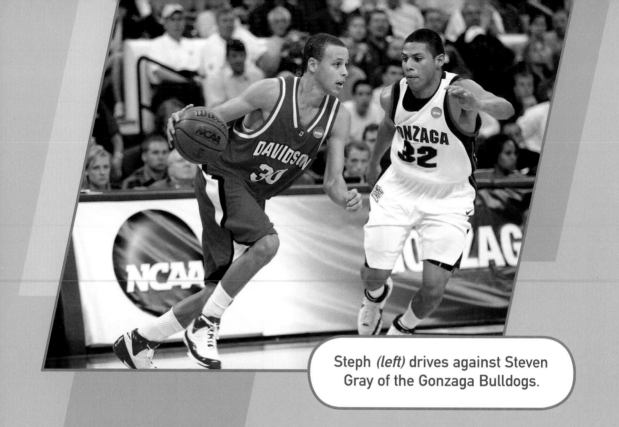

Steph *(left)* drives against Steven Gray of the Gonzaga Bulldogs.

WARRIOR

In the 2007–2008 season, Steph and the Wildcats made it to the NCAA tournament again. They were ranked 10th out of 16 **seeds** in their **region**. Steph made sure his team didn't lose in the first round, as they had the year before. He sank shot after shot. Steph scored 40 points, almost half his team's total! Davidson beat seventh-seeded Gonzaga University, 82–76.

In the next round, the Wildcats beat second-seeded Georgetown University, 74–70. Steph was the leading scorer on his team again with 30 points. In round 3, Steph scored 33 points and Davidson crushed the third-ranked University of Wisconsin, 73–56. The Wildcats had made it to the **Elite Eight**!

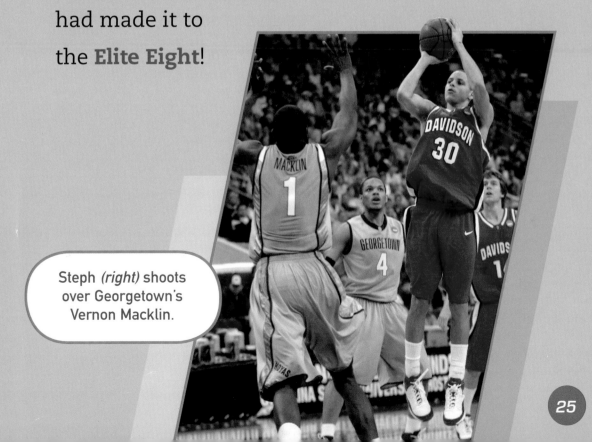

Steph *(right)* shoots over Georgetown's Vernon Macklin.

Steph had led his team to one unexpected victory after another. He became an instant star to basketball fans around the country.

Dell was overjoyed. "To see your son succeed and have fun on a national stage is great," Dell said.

The Wildcats' wild ride ended in their next game against the University of Kansas. Steph scored 25 points, but Kansas came out on top, 59–57. Kansas went on to win the tournament. "Not a lot of people expected a lot from us, so I'm proud of what we have accomplished," Steph said after the game. "But it hurts a lot to have been this close to the **Final Four.**"

In 2008–2009, Steph returned to Davidson for another shot at the Final Four. But the Wildcats didn't play as well as they had the previous year. They didn't win enough games to make it back to the NCAA tournament at the end of the season. Steph decided it was time to move on to the NBA. On June 25, 2009, the Golden State Warriors chose Steph with the seventh overall pick in the NBA **draft**. The Warriors play in Oakland, California.

Steph *(right)* shoots against New York Knicks guard Langston Galloway.

Steph *(right)* poses for
a photo with a fan.

Steph was named Most Valuable Player (MVP) by the NBA for his play in the 2014-2015 season. He has gotten used to going beyond people's expectations on the basketball court. "Everyone has opinions," he said. "All you can do is play your position, do what you can to help the team out, and continue to get better. . . . It's a good feeling when you get better."

Selected Career Highlights

2014–2015   Named Most Valuable Player (MVP) by the NBA
Voted to the NBA All-Star Game for the second time

2013–2014   Voted to the NBA All-Star Game for the first time
Ranked first in the NBA with 261 three-point field goals
Ranked sixth in the NBA with 1,873 points scored

2012–2013   Ranked first in the NBA with 272 three-point field goals
Ranked seventh in the NBA with 1,786 points scored

2011–2012   Played in only 26 games due to an ankle injury

2010–2011   Ranked 10th in the NBA with 151 three-point field goals

2009–2010   Ranked sixth in the NBA with 166 three-point field goals

2008–2009   Ranked second in the Southern Conference with 130 three-point field goals
Ranked fifth in the NCAA with 130 three-point field goals
Ranked first in the Southern Conference with 974 points scored
Ranked first in the NCAA with 974 points scored

2007–2008   Led Davidson to the Elite Eight in the NCAA tournament
Ranked first in the Southern Conference with 162 three-point field goals
Ranked first in the NCAA with 162 three-point field goals
Ranked first in the Southern Conference with 931 points scored
Ranked first in the NCAA with 931 points scored

2006–2007   Ranked first in the Southern Conference with 122 three-point field goals
Ranked third in the NCAA with 122 three-point field goals
Ranked first in the Southern Conference with 730 points scored

Glossary

conference: a group of teams that play against one another

defender: a player whose job is to stop the other team from scoring

draft: a yearly event in which teams take turns choosing new players from a group

dribble: to advance the ball by bouncing it

Elite Eight: the final eight teams remaining in the NCAA basketball tournament

Final Four: the final four teams remaining in the NCAA basketball tournament

full-court press: an aggressive style of play in which defenders cover the entire court, not just the area near their basket

National Collegiate Athletic Association (NCAA): the group that oversees college basketball

pick-and-roll: a play in which a player stands in place to set a pick, allowing another player on his team to take an open shot

region: one of the four groups of teams that make up the NCAA basketball tournament. The winner of each region plays in the Final Four.

scholarship: money awarded to students to help pay for college

scouts: basketball experts who watch players closely to judge their abilities

seeds: numbers assigned to teams in a tournament that rank the teams based on how likely they are to win

three-point field goals: shots made from behind the three-point line on a basketball court

tip-off: starting a new period in basketball by tossing the ball in the air between two opponents

tournament: a set of games held to decide the best team

varsity: the top team at a school

walk-on: a college athlete who tries out for a team with no offer of a scholarship

Further Reading & Websites

Gitlin, Marty. *Playing Pro Basketball*. Minneapolis: Lerner Publications, 2015.

Kennedy, Mike, and Mark Stewart. *Swish: The Quest for Basketball's Perfect Shot*. Minneapolis: Millbrook Press, 2009.

NBA
http://www.nba.com
The NBA's official website provides fans with recent news stories, statistics, biographies of players and coaches, and information about games.

Sports Illustrated Kids
http://www.sikids.com
The *Sports Illustrated Kids* website covers all sports, including basketball.

Stephen Curry 30
http://stephencurry30.com
Visit Steph's official website to view photos of Steph, learn about upcoming events, and much more.

Expand learning beyond the printed book. Download free, complementary educational resources for this book from our website, www.lerneresource.com.

Index

Photo Acknowledgments

The images in this book are used with the permission of: AP Photo/Marcio Jose Sanchez, pp. 4, 5, 6, 8; Seth Poppel Yearbook Library, pp. 9, 11, 12, 15, 16, 17, 19, 20; AP Photo/Fred Jewell, p. 10; Lee K. Marriner/UPI Photo Service/Newscom, p. 13; © iStockphoto.com/Tony Tremblay, p. 14; AP Photo/Chuck Burton, p. 17; © Davis Turner/Bloomberg/Getty Images, p. 21; Tim Cowie/icon SME AAE/Newscom, p. 22 (left); AP Photo/Duane Burleson, p. 22 (right); AP Photo/Michael Conroy, p. 23; © Kevin C. Cox/Getty Images, p. 24; AP Photo/Chuck Burton, pp. 25, 29; AP Photo/Jeff Chiu, p. 27; AP Photo/David Zalubowski, p. 28.

Front cover: Jose Carlos Fajardo/Bay Area News Group/TNS/Newscom.

Main body text set in Caecilia LT Std 55 Roman 16/28.
Typeface provided by Adobe Systems.